W9-ASD-333

ZOOS

GREAT PLACES TO VISIT

Jason Cooper

The Rourke Corporation, Inc.
Vero Beach, Florida 32964

Edited by Sandra A. Robinson

PHOTO CREDITS
© Lynn M. Stone: Cover, title page, pages 4, 7, 8, 10, 12, 15, 17, 18;
© James P. Rowan: pages 13, 21

ACKNOWLEDGEMENTS
The author thanks the following for their cooperation in the prepara-
tion of this book: Brookfield Zoo, Chicago, IL; Center for the Study of
Tropical Birds, San Antonio, TX; Cincinnati Zoo, Cincinnati, OH;
Lincoln Park Zoo, Chicago, IL; Lone Pine Koala Sanctuary,
Brisbane, Queensland, Australia; Lowry Park Zoo, Tampa, FL; San
Diego Zoo, San Diego, CA; Tallahassee Junior Museum,
Tallahassee, FL

LIBRARY OF CONGRESS
Library of Congress Cataloging-in-Publication Data
Cooper, Jason, 1942-
      Zoos / by Jason Cooper.
      p. cm. — (Great places to visit)
      Includes index.
      Summary: Briefly describes how zoos collect, care for, exhibit,
study, and teach about different kinds of animals.
      ISBN 0-86593-212-3
      1. Zoos—Juvenile literature. 2. Zoo animals—Juvenile literature.
[1. Zoos. 2. Zoo animals.] I. Title. II. Series: Cooper, Jason, 1942-
Great places to visit.
QL76.C66 1992
590'.74'4—dc20   92-12555
                                                                CIP
                                                                AC

TABLE OF CONTENTS

ZOOS

You may never see a wild tiger in India or a lion in Africa. But on a visit to the zoo you can see these and many other kinds of wild animals.

Zoos are places that show, or **exhibit,** wild animals from all over the world. Some zoos also have outstanding gardens.

Giraffe looks for handouts

ANIMALS AT THE ZOO

If you visit a large zoo, you will see hundreds of animals. Many will be in pairs, herds or flocks.

You will find an alphabet of animals, from antelopes to zebras. And there will be surprises, animals you never dreamed of—gibbons, guars, and gyrfalcons, oryxes, okapis and onagers.

*One of the zoo's great surprises—
a colorful (king) vulture!*

SPECIALTY ZOOS

Small zoos are often "specialty" zoos. They do not have as much room or as many animals as big city zoos. However, they often have fine **collections,** or groups, of certain kinds of animals.

The zoo at the Tallahassee Junior Museum in Florida, for example, shows only animals from Florida. The Alpenzoo in Austria exhibits only animals from the Alps Mountains.

Endangered Florida panther at the Tallahassee Junior Museum Zoo

EXHIBITS

You will see many zoo animals exhibited in outdoor homes, or exhibits. New zoos are careful to build exhibits that are something like an animal's **habitat,** its home in the wild. Such exhibits are known as habitat exhibits. They are often roomy and easy to view.

Instead of a cage's steel bars, waterways, trenches and glass are used to keep people and animals apart in modern zoos.

People can almost go nose-to-nose with tigers, bears and leopards in glass-walled exhibits.

Only glass separates curious sloth bear and curious kids

Koala mother and baby share a eucalyptus branch

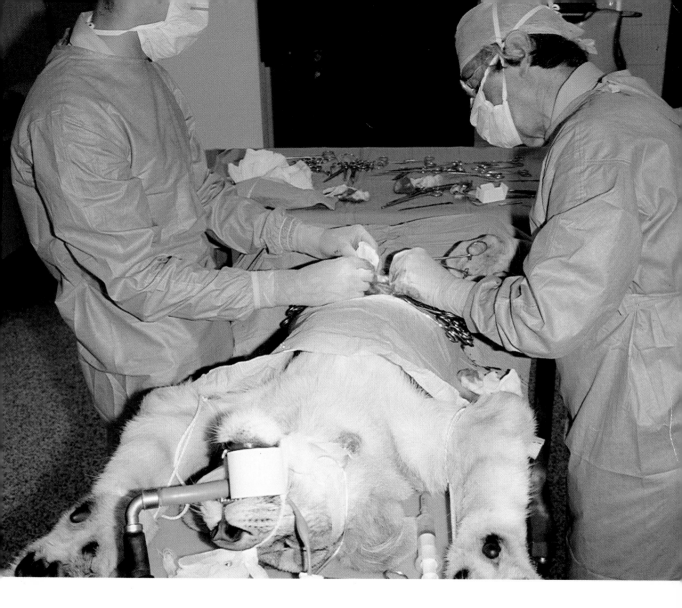

King of beasts gets royal treatment from zoo vets

STUDYING ANIMALS AT THE ZOO

When you visit the zoo, take time to watch how the animals behave. People who work at the zoo may also be studying the animals. Zoo workers watch some animals very closely to learn more about their behavior.

By studying animals in **captivity,** zoo workers can make better decisions about how to care for them. The zoo also learns more about how animals act in the wild. That is important, too, because zoos often take part in programs to protect wild animals.

Often studied wolf pack at Chicago's Brookfield Zoo

SAVING ANIMALS

Many kinds of animals at the zoo are **endangered** in the wild. They are in danger of disappearing altogether, of becoming **extinct.** Among them are tigers, leopards, rhinoceroses, gorillas, elephants and dozens of others.

Almost all of the animals at the zoo were born in a zoo somewhere. Zoos make a special effort to raise endangered animals. Some endangered animals raised by zoos can be released into the wild.

Endangered gorilla raised in captivity

TEACHING ABOUT ANIMALS

Zoos help you learn about animals in many ways. You can study animals' behavior and read about them on interesting signs.

Zoo signs tell many facts about animals, including if an animal is endangered.

Zoo education departments offer special programs and chances for people to see animals out of their exhibits.

Zoo libraries and bookstores also help teach about animals.

*Training an endangered
Asian elephant*

ZOOKEEPERS

Many of the workers at the zoo are keepers. Zookeepers clean animal exhibits, make sure the animals appear healthy, and feed them. Food for the animals is prepared in the zoo kitchen.

Some zookeepers are also animal **trainers.** They work with such animals as elephants, porpoises and hawks. Trained animals are used in zoo programs that show some of the animals' special abilities.

Zookeeper feeds a California sea lion

THE ZOO HOSPITAL

Zoos try to keep their animals strong and healthy. But like people, animals do become ill.

The zoo hospital is staffed by animal doctors called **veterinarians,** or "vets." A zoo veterinarian may treat an elephant one day and a baby bird the next.

When a big animal cannot be safely moved to the hospital, a vet treats it in the exhibit.

Glossary

captivity (kap TIHV ih tee) — the condition of being kept in a controlled place

collection (kuhl EX shun) — the group or groups of animals kept by a zoo

endangered (en DANE jerd) — in danger of disappearing altogether

exhibit (ex IHB it) — a zoo animal and its surroundings; the act of showing an animal (to exhibit)

extinct (ex TINKT) — no longer existing

habitat (HAB uh tat) — the kinds of places animals live, such as forests or deserts (zoo exhibits often recreate the animals' natural habitats)

trainer (TRAY ner) — one whose job is to teach, or train, certain actions to animals

veterinarian (veh trihn AIR ee uhn) — an animal doctor

INDEX